WE SHALL OVERCOME

VOICES OF THE CIVIL RIGHTS MOVEMENT

A PRIMARY SOURCE EXPLORATION OF THE STRUGGLE FOR RACIAL EQUALITY

by Lori Mortensen

Consultant:
Lyde Cullen Sizer, PhD
Professor of U.S. Cultural and Intellectual History
Sarah Lawrence College
Bronxville, New York

CAPSTONE PRESS
a capstone imprint

Fact Finders Books are published by Capstone Press,
1710 Roe Crest Drive, North Mankato, Minnesota 56003
www.capstonepub.com

Library of Congress Cataloging-in-Publication Data
Mortensen, Lori, 1955–
    Voices of the civil rights movement / Lori Mortensen.
        pages cm.—(Fact finders. We shall overcome)
    Summary: "The civil rights movement brought about major changes in the United States, including the legal end of
segregation between African-Americans and white Americans. Explore the points of view of the activists who fought
for change and the people who opposed them through powerful primary sources and historical photos"— Provided by
publisher.
    Includes bibliographical references and index.
    ISBN 978-1-4914-2044-7 (library binding)
    ISBN 978-1-4914-2219-9 (paperback)
    ISBN 978-1-4914-2234-2 (ebook PDF)
1. African Americans—Civil rights—History—20th century—Juvenile literature. 2. Civil rights movements—Southern
States--History—20th century—Juvenile literature. 3. Southern States—Race relations—Juvenile literature. I. Title.
    E185.61.M87 2015
    323.1196'073075—dc23   2014019814

Editorial Credits
Adrian Vigliano, editor; Cynthia Akiyoshi, designer; Wanda Winch, media researcher; Gene Bentdahl, production specialist

Photo Credits
AP Images, 14, Bill Hudson, 20, Horace Cort, 21; Arkansas Democrat-Gazette: cover (newspaper background); Corbis:
Bettmann, 9, 24, Hulton-Deutsch Collection, 13, Jack Moebes, 7, Steve Shapiro, 27; Getty Images: The LIFE Images
Collection/Don Cravens, cover (left), 8, 10, 11, The LIFE Picture Collection/Grey Villet, 23; LBJ Library: Yoichi Okamoto, 28;
Library of Congress: Prints and Photographs Division, cover (bottom, right), 4, 5, 6, 15, 16, 17, 18, 22, 25; Newscom: KRT, 26,
Zuma Press/The Commercial Appeal, 19; U.S. Air Force photo: MSgt. Cecilio Ricardo, 29

Printed in Canada.
092014   008478FRS15

A NOTE ABOUT PRIMARY SOURCES

Primary sources are newspaper articles, photographs, speeches, or
other documents that were created during an event. They are great
ways to see how people spoke and felt during that time. You'll find
primary sources from the time of the civil rights movement throughout
this book. Within the text, these primary sources are colored blue and

TABLE OF CONTENTS

Chapter One

SEPARATE AND NOT EQUAL

In 1865, toward the end of the Civil War (1861–1865), the 13th Amendment to the U.S. Constitution **abolished** slavery. In 1868 the 14th Amendment promised equal rights to all citizens. But these new laws did not erase more than 200 years of racial hatred and **prejudice** toward black people.

After the war southern states made "Jim Crow" laws. These laws separated black people from white people. Blacks had to sit in the backs of buses and trains. Blacks had to use separate facilities that were usually old and run-down. Many businesses refused to serve nonwhite citizens.

▶ Under Jim Crow laws, black or "colored" people were not treated like equal citizens.

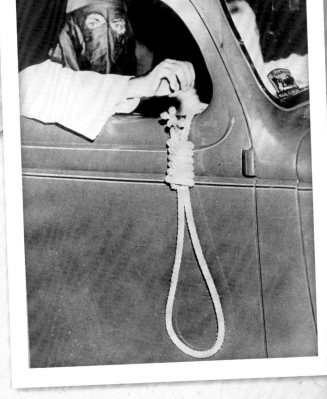

A National Crime

Black people who broke **segregation** rules could be fined and arrested. Sometimes black people were attacked or even killed by mobs. Guilt or innocence did not matter. Instead of going to trial, white mobs killed blacks at public **lynchings**.

During the 1890s Ida B. Wells, a black journalist, spoke out against these brutal killings. She even met with President William McKinley. *"Our country's national crime is lynching,"* she said. More people began speaking up and taking action to challenge segregation. People who supported segregation spoke up too. The fight over civil rights seemed to grow louder every day.

abolish—to put an end to something officially

prejudice—an opinion about others that is unfair or not based on facts

segregate—to keep people of different races apart in schools and other public places

lynch—to be killed by a mob without a trial, usually by hanging

Chapter Two

TIRED OF GIVING IN

On December 1, 1955, in Montgomery, Alabama, Rosa Parks got on a bus. Jim Crow laws said black passengers had to sit in the back. If the bus filled up, they had to give up their seats to white passengers.

That day, a white passenger needed a seat. The driver told Parks to get up. Parks recalled her confrontation with the bus driver, *"When he saw me still sitting, he asked if I was going to stand up and I said, 'No, I'm not.' And he said, 'Well, if you don't stand up, I'm going to have to call the police and have you arrested.' I said, 'You may do that.'"*

▶ Rosa Parks' arrest was the event that started the Montgomery Bus Boycott.

Parks was arrested for *"refusing to obey orders of bus driver."* Local black leaders learned of Parks' actions. They asked all black people to **boycott** the buses in Montgomery. Thousands of people stopped riding the buses. Some of the leaders formed a group called the Montgomery Improvement Association (MIA) to coordinate the boycott.

Some people claimed Parks didn't get up because she was tired. *"No, the only tired I was,"* Parks explained, *"was tired of giving in."*

boycott—to refuse to take part in something as a way of making a protest

FACT

Many call Rosa Parks the mother of the civil rights movement.

Chapter Three
THEY CAN WALK

Clyde Sellers was the Police Commissioner of Montgomery in 1955. When black people boycotted city buses, he vowed to arrest anyone who broke segregation rules.

"You know," said Sellers during an interview, *"the Nigras in Montgomery were treated better than any place else. They got everything from the whites—they went to the whites for everything they wanted and they got it ... [the whites] don't want to do it anymore."*

▶ During the boycott protesters found other ways to travel. Many people rode bicylces, found carpools, or simply walked.

Sellers saw only one solution. *"We have laws requiring segregation on the buses, and if they want to ride the buses they will have to obey the laws. They can walk until they are ready to obey the law."*

The bus boycott went on for 12 months. One night in early 1956 boycott leader Martin Luther King Jr.'s home was bombed. After the bombing Sellers met with King and said, *"I will certainly do everything in my power to bring the guilty parties to court and put them in prison ... I do not agree with you in your beliefs, but I will do everything within my power to defend you against such acts as this."*

Chapter Four

FATHER OF THE CIVIL RIGHTS MOVEMENT

Following Rosa Parks' arrest, local black leaders gathered to plan a boycott. During this meeting the MIA was formed, and a young minister named Martin Luther King Jr. was appointed president of the organization.

King agreed to lead a bus boycott to protest inequality. On December 5, 1955, King spoke to a crowd of thousands of boycotters. He urged people to use carpools and other options to stay off the buses until they reached their goal.

▶ Boycott leaders organized a carpool system for people to use instead of buses.

King told the crowd, "*Automobiles will be at your service ... Now my automobile is gonna be in it ... and I'm not concerned about how much gas I'm gonna use. I want to see this thing work. And we will not be content until oppression is wiped out of Montgomery, and really out of America.*"

Police arrested 26-year-old King for leading the boycott. It was the first time King received national attention for his work in the civil rights movement.

King's voice became a powerful force in Montgomery. Under his leadership, the boycott gained national attention. Soon lawyers were arguing for and against bus segregation in front of the Supreme Court.

In November 1956 the Supreme Court struck down laws requiring segregated seating on public buses. The boycotters had won.

"I Have a Dream"

After leading the bus boycott in Montgomery, King became a major leader in the civil rights movement. He worked with other leaders to organize nonviolent protests to fight against segregation.

On August 28, 1963, more than 250,000 people marched in Washington, D.C.

"I have a dream," King said in his speech to the crowd, *"that my four little children will one day live in a nation where they will not be judged by the color of their skin, but by the content of their character."*

King shared his vision of the future. He imagined the day, *"when all of God's children, black men and white men, Jews and Gentiles, Protestants and Catholics, will be able to join hands and sing in the words of the old Negro spiritual: Free at last, Free at last, Great God a-mighty, We are free at last!"*

King's powerful words rang in the nation's ears. His speech inspired people to keep fighting for civil rights.

Suffering for the Cause

King suffered many assaults and arrests during his fight for civil rights. On April 4, 1968, King was shot and killed while standing on a motel balcony in Memphis, Tennessee. His friend and fellow civil rights leader, Ralph Abernathy, was by his side. *"I have suffered as much as Martin Luther King,"* said Abernathy. *"Only I didn't get the bullet. And I would have taken the bullet if I could have."*

Chapter Five

BY ANY MEANS NECESSARY

After a lifetime of **discrimination**, Malcolm X grew impatient with injustice. He rallied blacks to fight racism, *"by any means necessary"* and called Martin Luther King Jr. a *"fool."*

King believed peaceful protest was an effective tool. Malcolm X believed nonviolent protests taught blacks to be defenseless. While King fought for integration, Malcolm X fought for blacks to live separately and govern themselves.

"I am a Muslim," said Malcolm X, *"because it's a religion that teaches you an eye for an eye and a tooth for a tooth. It teaches you to respect everybody, and treat everybody right. But it also teaches you if someone steps on your toe, chop off their foot. And I carry my religious axe with me all the time."*

▶ Malcolm X held up a newspaper while addressing a crowd in New York City in 1963. He encouraged blacks not to wait to get involved in the fight for equal rights.

▶ Malcolm X and King met only once, as King was leaving a press conference in March of 1964. Malcolm X died less than one year later—he was assassinated on February 21, 1965.

Malcolm X's revolutionary stand against injustice united blacks all over the world—and created enemies. His message frightened white society. Some people in the black community thought violence would damage the progress made through peaceful protests.

Some of Malcolm X's views changed over time. In 1964 Malcolm X said he wanted to find ways to work with other civil rights leaders. He said, *"Dr. King wants the same thing I want—freedom!"*

discriminate—to treat people unfairly because of their skin color or class

Chapter Six

ARGUING FOR FREEDOM

Thurgood Marshall's words hushed the courtroom. He said that the real reason for continuing to have segregated schools was to keep people who had been slaves *"as near that stage as is possible."* He concluded by saying, *"this Court should make it clear that that is not what our Constitution stands for."*

In 1952 Marshall began arguing a case before the Supreme Court for a group of black families. These families did not want their children forced to attend a black school far from their homes. This case, *Brown v. Board of Education,* challenged a ruling from 1896 that said "separate but equal" was constitutional.

▶ The Supreme Court's *Brown* decision provided a legal basis for the civil rights movement over the next 10 years.

FACT

In 1967 Marshall became the first black person to serve on the Supreme Court.

▶ Marshall served for 24 years on the Supreme Court. He died in 1993 at the age of 84.

On May 14, 1954, the Supreme Court agreed with Marshall. *"... in the field of public education,"* wrote Chief Justice Earl Warren, *"... separate educational facilities are inherently unequal."* The ruling cleared the way for school **integration**. This was a huge victory for the civil rights movement.

Historian Roger Wilkins remembered Marshall by saying, *"Segregation was crushing; It crushed black people's belief that what they said and did and thought counted for something. Thurgood Marshall led a team of lawyers before an all-white court and gave us one of the three or four most important constitutional decisions this country has ever seen."*

integrate—to bring people of different races together in schools and other public places

Chapter Seven

NOT AS LONG AS I AM GOVERNOR

The Supreme Court's 1955 ruling to integrate public schools outraged many people in the South. While some states began taking steps to integrate, many refused and made laws against integration. In 1957 a federal court ordered Little Rock, Arkansas to comply with the 1955 decision. The school board began by enrolling nine black students at Central High School. The students were called the Little Rock Nine.

Governor Orval Faubus decided to fight school integration. He knew a big fight would help him win an upcoming election. Faubus said, *"No school district will be forced to mix the races as long as I am governor of Arkansas."*

▶ Faubus went on TV to ask voters to support his stand against integration.

AGAINST RACIAL INTEGRATION OF ALL SCHOOLS WITHIN THE LITTLE ROCK SCHOOL DISTRICT...

▶ One of the Little Rock Nine, Elizabeth Eckford, walked to school as angry white protestors followed her.

The day before school started, Faubus ordered the Arkansas National Guard to surround the school. *"It will not be possible,"* he explained during a televised speech, *"to ... maintain order and protect the lives and property of the citizens if forcible integration is carried out."* Faubus later won the election and served six terms in a row. *"It's true in politics as it is in life,"* he said, *"that survival is the first law."*

Chapter Eight

SEGREGATION AT ALL COSTS

Martin Luther King Jr. called Birmingham, Alabama, *"the most segregated city in the United States."* That was exactly how the city's commissioner of public safety, Eugene "Bull" Connor, wanted to keep it. *"Negroes and whites will not segregate together as long as I am commissioner,"* he declared.

Civil rights leaders knew Birmingham was an important battleground. On May 2, 1963, more than 1,000 children marched through the streets singing freedom songs. To turn them back, Connor brought out fire hoses and police dogs. The hose blasts knocked marchers to the ground. The dogs lunged and bit.

▶ Images from Birmingham shocked people around the country. It was a major turning point for civil rights.

▶ Connor (center) directed the arrest of a group of black demonstrators on April 10, 1963.

Photos from Birmingham outraged many Americans and exposed the battle for civil rights like never before. *"... the water ripped clothing and sent children rolling down the street,"* said a reporter.

Connor's violent methods made some Americans sympathetic to the goals of the civil rights movement. President Kennedy proposed legislation that would lead to the Civil Rights Act of 1964 that banned discrimination. *"The civil rights movement should thank God for Bull Connor,"* said Kennedy. *"He's helped it as much as Abraham Lincoln."*

Chapter Nine

HATE CAN DESTROY YOU

After three white men murdered her mother, Daisy Bates hated white people. Her father said, *"Hate can destroy you. Don't hate white people just because they're white ... Hate the humiliations ... discrimination ... the insults hurled at us—and then try to do something about it."*

Bates did do something.

In 1957 she was a leader in the local chapter of the National Association for the Advancement of Colored People (NAACP). She fought for school integration. She became an adviser to the nine black students who would enroll at Central High School in Little Rock, Arkansas.

▶ Daisy Bates (back row, second from right) posed for a picture with the Little Rock Nine.

▶ Hate groups broke Bates' front window. She fixed the glass with tape and kept fighting for equality.

Hate groups burned crosses on Bates' lawn as an act of intimidation. A rock with the note, *"Stone this time. Dynamite next"* shattered her window. But she was determined to keep fighting for civil rights.

"I never know when they're going to pass here and blow this house to bits," she said, *" ... nevertheless, I feel if I'm going to live in this town and with myself, I must oppose hatred and prejudice in any way that I can."*

Chapter Ten

IF NOT US, THEN WHO?

On May 20, 1961, a group of Freedom Riders sat together on a bus as it rolled toward Montgomery, Alabama. The group was heading to a segregated bus terminal. Freedom Riders were civil rights activists who rode buses into the South. They rode in mixed racial groups to challenge segregation on interstate buses.

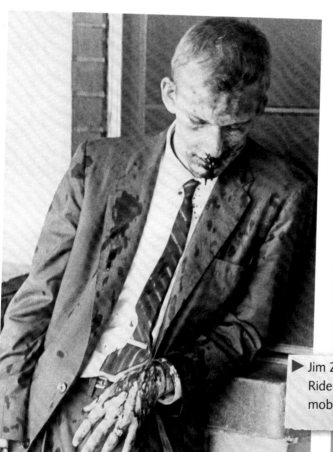

One Freedom Rider, Genevieve Houghton, said, *"We were to go through various parts of the South, gradually going deeper and deeper ... and see whether places were segregated, whether people were being served when they went to get something to eat, or buy a ticket, or use the restrooms."*

▶ Jim Zwerg was one Freedom Rider who was attacked by a mob in Montgomery.

▶ A journalist snapped photos of John Lewis and Zwerg beaten by the mob. Their bloodied faces were shown around the world.

When a bus of Freedom Riders arrived in Montgomery, an enraged mob attacked with bats and pipes. Police arrived about 10 minutes later. They did almost nothing to stop the mob's attack.

But the movement grew and hundreds of people became Freedom Riders. *"If not us, then who?"* said Freedom Rider John Lewis. *"If not now, then when?"*

On September 22, 1961, the Interstate Commerce Commission outlawed discrimination on interstate buses and at bus stations. The Freedom Riders had achieved their goal.

Chapter Eleven

SEGREGATION FOREVER

In 1962 George Wallace ran for governor of Alabama. Many voters in Alabama liked Wallace and they showed it with their votes. He spoke against black voting rights and school integration. He won the election.

After his election Wallace gave his inaugural address. He said, *"I draw the line in the dust ... I say segregation now, segregation tomorrow, segregation forever."*

In March 1965, about 600 peaceful civil rights demonstrators began marching from Selma to Montgomery, Alabama. Wallace ordered state troopers to stop them.

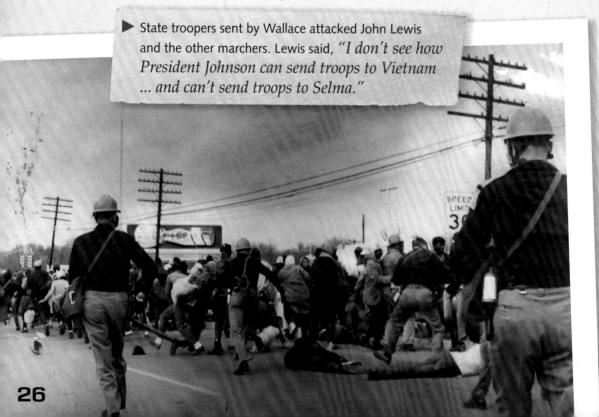

▶ State troopers sent by Wallace attacked John Lewis and the other marchers. Lewis said, *"I don't see how President Johnson can send troops to Vietnam ... and can't send troops to Selma."*

In 1963 Wallace stood in the doorway of a University of Alabama building. He was trying to stop two black students from enrolling.

Alabama state troopers met the demonstrators at the Edmund Pettus Bridge. When the marchers refused to leave, troopers attacked with clubs, whips, and tear gas.

"All I remember is screaming," recalled marcher Joanne Bland. *"They ran those horses up into the crowd and were knocking people down ... Blood was everywhere."*

But Wallace did not apologize. He continued to speak out for segregation. He said, *"The president wants us to surrender this state to Martin Luther King and his group of pro-Communists who have instituted these demonstrations."*

Chapter Twelve

A CHANGING NATION

On July 2 President Johnson signed the Civil Rights Act of 1964. This outlawed discrimination in certain areas of public life, such as public education and accommodations. Congress ratified the 24th Amendment, eliminating poll taxes in federal elections that prevented many blacks from voting. The next year Johnson signed the Voting Rights Act of 1965, protecting blacks' right to vote.

Martin Luther King Jr. talked about the United States' beginning in his "I Have a Dream" speech. King said, *"When the architects of our republic wrote the magnificent words of the Constitution and the Declaration of Independence, they were signing a ... promise that all men—yes, black men as well as white men— would be guaranteed the 'unalienable rights' of 'life, liberty, and the pursuit of happiness.'"*

▶ President Johnson signed the Civil Rights Act of 1964 in a televised ceremony at the White House.

▶ On November 4, 2008, Barack Obama became the first African-American president of the United States. This would not have been possible without the courageous voices of the civil rights movement.

The people of the civil rights movement raised their voices to demand their rights. Slowly the nation began to change. Changes did not come easily, but they did come. People began thinking differently about discrimination. Opportunities for African-Americans increased. The changes of the civil rights movement affect people today and will affect generations to come.

Selected Bibliography

Bausum, Ann. *Freedom Riders: John Lewis and Jim Zwerg on the Front Lines of the Civil Rights Movement.* Washington, D.C.: National Geographic, 2006.

"City Threatens Arrests Here to Enforce Bus Segregation." *The Associated Press.* April 24, 1956. http://www.montgomeryboycott.com/city-threatens-arrests-here-to-enforce-bus-segregation/

Fine, Benjamin. "Arkansas Troops Bar Negro Pupils; Governor Defiant." *The New York Times.* September 5, 1957. http://www.nytimes.com/learning/general/onthisday/big/0904.html#article

Freedman, Russell. *Freedom Walkers: The Story of the Montgomery Bus Boycott.* New York: Holiday House, 2006.

Kasher, Steven. *The Civil Rights Movement Photographic History 1954-68.* New York: Abbeville Press, 1996.

"The Montgomery Bus Boycott: December 1955–December 1956." PBS/WGBH, August 23, 2006. http://www.pbs.org/wgbh/amex/eyesontheprize/story/02_bus.html

Partridge, Elizabeth. *Marching for Freedom: Walk Together, Children, and Don't You Grow Weary.* New York: Viking, 2009.

Van Delinder, Jean. "Brown v. Board of Education of Topeka: A Landmark Case Unresolved Fifty Years Later." *Prologue Magazine,* 2004. http://www.archives.gov/publications/prologue/2004/spring/brown-v-board-1.html

Walker, Paul Robert. *Remember Little Rock: The Time, the People, the Stories.* Washington, D.C.: National Geographic, 2009.

Williams, Juan. "Daisy Bates and the Little Rock Nine." NPR, September 21, 2007. http://www.npr.org/templates/story/story.php?storyId=14563865

Glossary

abolish (uh-BOL-ish)—to put an end to something officially

assassinate (us-SASS-uh-nate)—to murder a person who is well known or important

boycott (BOY-kot)—to refuse to take part in something as a way of making a protest

discriminate (dis-KRI-muh-nayt)—to treat people unfairly because of their skin color or class

integrate (IN-tuh-grate)—to bring people of different races together in schools and other public places

lynch (LINCH)—to put someone to death, often by hanging, by mob action without legal authority

prejudice (PREJ-uh-diss)—an opinion about others that is unfair or not based on facts

segregate (SEG-ruh-gate)—to keep people of different races apart in schools and other public places

Critical Thinking
Using the Common Core

1. Many activists were arrested or violently attacked during the civil rights movement. Discuss some of the reasons why people might accept great risks to take a stand for civil rights. (Key Ideas and Details)

2. Why do you think some people were so opposed to integration? Discuss the different reactions these people had. Were their reactions justified? Support your answer with examples from the text and other sources. (Integration of Knowledge and Ideas)

Internet Sites

FactHound offers a safe, fun way to find Internet sites related to this book. All of the sites on FactHound have been researched by our staff.

Here's all you do:
Visit *www.facthound.com*
Type in this code: 9781491420447

 Check out projects, games and lots more at
www.capstonekids.com

Index